"I started reading Michael Poage's *I Know Just What You Mean* at four in the morning. As it turned out it was a perfect time for espionage. Poem after poem, I began to feel like an agent from some metaphorical intelligence agency. Poage's images took me around the world, Bosnia, Turkey, Gaza. I spied into the hearts of the world's most innocent victims: mother's feeding children, changing diapers, old men marveling at how they've aged in crises, doctor's in hot zones laboring for the welfare of their patients. I found desert and ocean, books disappearing like dreams. Poage writes for those who cannot write for themselves. His poems tell the history of both trauma and hope. We can return to his words in the middle of the night."

        -Al Ortolani, author of *Controlled Burn* and *Bull in the Ring*

"The great Mexican poet, Octavio Paz, once said this: "In poetry, the world is seen as marvelous." I mention it because it applies to the poems of Michael Poage in his new and 18th (!) collection, *I Know Just What You Mean*. The word "marvelous" can mean not only *wonderful*, but also awe-inspiring or astonishing. These little astonishments show up in a poem like "The Edge," about grandparents taking their toddler grandchild to the sea. The poem ends with a startling pronouncement: we edge away from the dangers of the salt and sea / move inward to the questions of each / estuarial day.

Against these dangers, *I Know Just What You Mean* balances the marvelous with the stark realities – and horrors – of modern life. Poage goes where American poets too often fear to tread. Poage calls out official criminality. His poems refuse to look away from our recent and ongoing nightmares, the recent and ongoing genocide. He ends Habsora: Gaza, 2023 with an image that is both crushing and unforgivable: the four premature babies are / decomposing in hospital / the small coffins / are the heaviest.

I Know Just What You Mean is an important and essential work by a poet who gives us what we need: the marvelous and the stark truths. They are not incompatible. Rather, they tell the whole story, as recounted by a poet who serves as an acute, a more accurate historian, and a witness to our times. The poet Richard Hugo described the poet's art as "writing one's spiritual autobiography." That's what Michael Poage does in this collection. It's a profound and marvelous accomplishment."

    -Ed Harkness

ADDITIONAL COLLECTIONS OF POETRY
BY MICHAEL POAGE

Born, Black Stone Press, 1975

Handbook of Ornament, Black Stone Press, 1979

The Gospel of Mary, Woodley Press, 1997

god won't overlook us, Penthe Press, 2001

Abundance, 219 Press, 2004

Voice Over, Blue Cedar Press, 2012

And So It Goes, Blue Cedar Press, 2014

The Comedic Applicant, Blue Cedar Press, 2015

The Average Level of Happiness, Blue Cedar Press, 2016

Human Ink, Blue Cedar Press, 2017

Ain't Leav'n This House Rough-Dried, Spartan Press, 2019

An Incident That Might Lead To Something,
Spartan Press, 2020

You Must Have Your Famine, Spartan Press, 2021

Lies I've Heard or Told, Spartan Press, 2022

Why The Will To Punish, Spartan Press, 2023

Heart: Collected Poems, 1975-2024, Spartan Press, 2024

Essential Workers, Spartan Press, 2025

I KNOW JUST
WHAT YOU MEAN

Poems by

MICHAEL POAGE

Spartan
Press

Spartan Press

Kansas City, Missouri

spartanpresskc.com

Spartan
Press

Copyright © Michael Poage, 2026

First Edition: 1 3 5 7 9 10 8 6 4 2

ISBN: 979-8-89975-036-6

LCCN: 2026933637

Author photo: Dr. Gretchen Eick

Table of Contents

PART I

PART II

PART III

"You mean you think I'm a coward?"
"I didn't say that, Peter."
"But you meant that. Didn't you?"
"No. I didn't mean that. I didn't mean
Anything. Let's not fight."

-James Baldwin, GOING TO MEET THE MAN

To Nico - "Happy Birthday, Baba"

PART I

SECRET SERVICE

I chose not to respond
                    To your false
Hospitality.

The invitation card
            Itself
Betrays the words, 'would love

                    To celebrate with you' because my name
Is misspelled and
            Has an awkward
                                Font.

So, I chose
To stand in the background

                                As a lost child,

Or like a Secret Service
            Agent, whispering
Into my lapel.
                    I will stand
In the dark corner,
Hoping not to be noticed,
                    To remain

                    Alone, waiting for the

Perpetrator,
whispering to myself

Whispering to myself,
'Eagle' just left the nest with 'Starlet.'

INHERITED NOSTALGIA

I

You were told that old farmers saying,
'If you wash your right hand, the left
One will also be washed.' You were
Made to memorize it which was easy
And obvious. Why was that dirt farmers
Saying so unique or important? Is that
What is meant by inherited nostalgia?
If so, aren't there other, more meaningful
Examples?

II

JP Morgan Core Bond Fund, view
The summary prospectus, don't waste time,
Hurry to look at the prospectus. Does it tell
The future? Or is it a hooded figure in the dark
Giving you those nightmares? Or it
Could be the micro vascular
Disease slowly walking with you
At night offering to carry you away
Out the closest window.

III

My Surroundings #3 poem
Will come into the picture, soon, when it
Is written, and the poem will calm
My anxiety, my fear of the nostalgic,
All the stuff I inherited, passed on to
My children to fulfill their
Fears of all I left as their inheritance.

GRIEF

She constructs her own weather.
Then, depending on outside conditions, she waits.
It happens to be very hot,
In spite of which she is very mellow
Searching for the appreciation
Needed at such times. She says to me,
'No time or energy to talk to anyone.'
She has been diagnosed, has meds,
A therapist, as she makes her own weather,
Measures the distance between
Who she is and who she is to become,
Searching for the appreciation.

LETTERS FROM JACK SPICER

"Dear JoAnn,
I know just what you mean."

I know of Jack Spicer, died in 1960
at 40. Did most of his writing
in San Francisco. But does anyone here
know JoAnn? I do not but I am
curious. She could have been another
poet in Jack's circle of writers. Did he have
a circle of writers? You are probably
thinking, 'Google it!' But I want to maintain
this epistemological distance for now. Anyone
in this room want to help me, just raise your
hand if you have an idea. Not everyone
at once! Yes, you standing in the back.
What is your guess? Who is JoAnn?
'A lover?' That's a moderate possibility.
Remember, 'Your illness is your life.'
Someone said that and I just wanted
to pass it on to you. Is there another
try? Yes, you in the middle with
the Red Sox cap on. 'Maybe she is
his sister.?' Another moderate possibility
but you all are just punching in the
air. Really, for me this is a letter
to my wife whom I love. As we each
show signs of getting older: diabetes,
gut issues, daily exhaustion, micro vascular
disease. I am sneaking this note in

at the end of this poem. Because I want her to
know that as we are now in our eighties,
1.9% of the population of this country
serve in that army. We have to be excellent
snipers or clever pacifists and flee this land.
You were gone for six days, and I didn't like
being in this house alone. Let's make a pact
to always hold hands with each other
and say, 'I know just what you mean.'

POETRY BEGAN

The other way is wisdom.
The sand is native to the
Elders who walk rather than
Ride a carriage pulled
By four matched Belgians.

I will bet that poetry began
When God said, *"Don't go near that damn tree."*
W. B. Yeats was born on this day in 1865!!
We have the same compressed schedule
As last year. The sand is native to the elders.

Chair Mao was so admired but the
Sand was not his choice. His wisdom
Diminished. If you are looking for
A glimmer of hope, don't ask the agents,
They have no wisdom. Maybe Yeats.

Do not cross your fingers. You can celebrate
Yeats' birthday or the end of the U.S.
Civil War. Another human slaughter
To keep from the children. For salvation
Open up the desert, greetings from the desert Mothers.

INCOMMODING

In case of emergency
break glass
any glass within reach
then run for
your life
because constant neglect
is a form
of violence and domestic
violence you will want
to avoid then you
might want to
break something else if
he comes near you again
you remember your heart
is still beating
with the childlike energy you
admitted is fed by rage.

THE CELTIC LIFE

O boatman, o boatman where do you find
The time for the other things in life?

Do you make an effort to capture the fastidious
God of your soaking ancestors? I know the feeling

Of growing into and out of the flesh of faith,
And crawling around and over the pulpit,

A word coming from the one for "gallows."
Have you been caught in the wild waves of

The sea from Holyhead to Dublin and return
In the wild waves hitting you like betrayal

Testing your complex, elaborate mapping skills
Until the obvious swamping conclusion when

Those few who came with you try waking you
Up from your stern, exhausted stone-pillowed sleep?

CONFUSION #1

no address
for a month
got off at wrong
station (underground)
and got back on
for Paddington
weird names
and hotel
Piccadilly line
goes to Heathrow

takes an hour
can't get right change
Heathrow shuttle
connecting train
takes an hour
dinner
at Paddington
Pride pub

all I taste
is the stench
of the mass graves
surrounding us
and me trying to
identify the pelvic
bone I am holding

male or female

forever

no address

forever

MAYONNAISE

Somewhere in a neighborhood
in northern Virginia, buried
in the backyard of a house
is a mayonnaise jar with a
blue parakeet, dead, wrapped
in a piece of quilting fabric.
The night that he died I was
with some friends down the
street, two other guys and one
girl. We were lying in the grass
of a nearby park, looking at
the dark sky with all those
mysterious stars and the silence
when one of the boys reached
over and touched the girl between
her legs, like she expected it but not
like she enjoyed it. Then the other
one touched her where breasts
were beginning. Again, the girl
didn't stop them but she seemed
resigned to something that had
happened before, as if that's
why she was with us. She looked
at me and her eyes reminded me
of the eyes of the dying, I would
see much later in my life. And she
was wearing all black, a shirt and

jeans. In their quiet way, the boys
left. The girl stood up, brushed
the loose grass from her black
clothes, and walked silently
away, sad, and alone under dim
streetlights. I took a last glance
at the stars, and went my own
way home thinking of a black
shirt and jeans. I found the blue
parakeet lying dead on the floor of the cage.

A VERY SMOOTH LANDING

It was an easy flight
From Zagreb to Sarajevo.
I had the window seat
With an empty middle and a
Young mother with a one-year
Old or so boy on the aisle.
I could see she would welcome
Help with her son and she was tired.
We talked some with her spotty
English and my poor Bosnian.
I found out she was from Croatia
And her husband was working
Out of country. She had
An apartment in the city of Mostar, my
Ultimate destination also, I told her.
Between managing her abundant
Blond hair and holding on to her understandably
Squirrelly son, I offered to help.
Afterall, I had two great grandchildren,
All that experience which I didn't mention.
We laid her child on the middle
Seat for a diaper change as his mother told me
About a difficult marriage, maybe done.
After a very smooth landing, she thanked
Me for my help. Then gave me a piece of
Paper with her local phone number on it
And suggested she could be my girl in Mostar.

PART II

why?

why do we stand
like birds stranded
on the beach

you touch my arm
my face
as if we were not alone

SEAGULLS

So, to let you know
The sky here is full
Of ash because of the
Constant shelling and fires.

My patient's lungs are
Suffering the shadow
Syndrome causing breathing
Difficulty and tumors.

Everyone with any strength
Writes their memoir with
Longings for the salt air
Of any sea to wash

Over them, or to die.
Seagulls, conjured by the
Imaginations of the sick,
Snagged the splintered

Bones of the washed up,
The done for, making another
Meal. So, to let you know
The sky here is full, very.

IS WAR ITSELF A CRIME?

-        *Washington Post headline*

Some of my best friends tell me
These are the greatest times. We are free
To dig the ditches, drain the marshes,
Build the cheap dream home. And we are all odd
In our own spectacular, low brow, manipulative,
Or generous ways. Still, we point out to each other
The strangeness we display when we finally can
Thank god no charges were filed in that assault
That you and I were clearly shown as inflamed. And I
        would
Do the same if faced with that ugly and expensive
        sometimes
Religious status with our own facial features,
Just a full blank stare as we are surrounded
By the crimes themselves. An independent investigation
Is just starting to examine the bones and shreds of
        clothing,
Forensic experts will determine the true crime.

KRAKOW, TENNESSEE

it doesn't matter
the pale concrete
a dance on the ancient
streets of stone
like in Memphis
the Lorraine Motel
the room with King
throwing pillows
at friends like
little kids
the cars in the lot
the friends going
to dinner at
rev. kyles' house
wish I was there
i have some questions
about the words
on the street
the scandal
from the skin down
you can hide
in Krakow only
until the arrow
finds you

PHOTO

The tool
of moaning
for the man.
Entanglements,
now eyes
closed.

A photograph
is always
a glance
at the real,
the crawling,
the presumed
suicide in
Pasadena.

Pleasant magnum
of abundance
as we promised
a silence, a still shot
like brothers
mingling the sad blood.

THE TORNADO HYATT

Whenever I step out my front door
The two dogs across the street, behind
A gate, bark and bark as if
I am challenging their existence on
This prairie boulevard. Just vicious
Attempts to do the most to hold on to minority
Power, just old-fashioned fear.
Then you tell me about the world's
First space hotel, ready for occupancy
In 2027. I respond with, 'Ok, but
How will the hot tub work?' In the
Grey dust of a coming storm, my
Real question – as the horizon begins
To disappear, is just that. 'In ____
Years, will that horizon have already
Taken me in, introduced me around?'

FLESH WOUND

I just found out that the brain uses
Up calories. You all knew that, right,
Having paid attention in biology class?
I knew some things and enjoyed
The dissection of the frog more
Than most. But I am now distracted
By the lace curtains in my study
And the feral pink sky as the sun
Sets, as usual, in the west. In such
A distraction I lose focus on my job
Here on the front lines. I am a lousy soldier
And pay for it. Medics called it a flesh wound.
But I think it was more serious.
Tell me…how many calories do I have left?

BLIND OUTLET #2

I have forgotten
those times
others call
memorable. My
most intimate
mysteries, simply
not knowing when
to stop,
slight,
hurtful,
and up to my waist
in fresh snow
looking like
a Montana calendar
photo. I simply
didn't know
when to stop.

WALKING

The river is low.
Why is that? you ask,
just as I was
wondering the
same thing.
Once in a while,
two angels
collide to make
a glad day.

VIBURNUM

Most of these flowers
are unscented
but those that are fragrant
are wonderfully so.
If it doesn't rain
at least an inch
a week
the plant needs
to be watered.
It is meant
for an outdoor life
with sun, some shade
but remember the most
your love
fragrant and wonderfully so.

Utah

little leaguer
makes
a ridiculous
diving
snag

LEAVES

– *For Nico*

Let's gather the leaves together.
I will exchange some of mine
for some of yours. I like
the red and the orange ones. Which
are your favorites? Do you
collect the leaves for fun or
are you some secret scientist genius
not even two years old? Just
asking. Other items will become
the object of your curiosity, perhaps
the river flowing this ancient bridge
but beautiful in all the ways

you will learn. Where did I go
when I said goodbye? Every
grief brings on every other
grief. You cry, and I cry.
There is no helpful answer to your
question. I find the leaves
you gave me in my shirt pocket.
Under two or three receipts
and a candy wrapper. The leaves
are dry and crushed in pieces.
I am sorry I did not take
better care of your leaves,
They were your gift to me and

I did not cherish them. I just
Crushed them into smaller pieces.
Beware the one who
accepts your beautiful gifts
and stuffs them in a pocket.

HYBRID VIGOR

She's is a noisy lover
                                but that is not her only
endearing quality.
                There is the hacking cough and the loud
lectures on Charles and
            Elaine Eastman, the shameful U.S. Indigenous
policy of the late 19th century,
                                and conversations in the night
she refuses to let me enter.
                                I wonder how often we get
the answer but does the compass
                of the vigor point clearly to the truth?
And the tense of the hybrid
                                grammar or the tension
of her daily life is not quiet
                        as when she when she mentions
her next book and the chapters
                        that just disappeared
or appear to have
        from her computer. I know what has happened
and her frustration
                lands in the middle of the living room
like an AIRBUS A330
                        at Heathrow.

no sign of the worm

turning, the war
ending, or a breath
taken. the toxic tide
bathes the beach
and the swimming children
with poison while
in bethlehem
christmas celebrations are
canceled. my country
continues supplying
the oppressor
with illegal weapons
for the immiseration.
jesus is born
in the rubble.

HABSORA

—   Gaza, 2023

The sun is

blocked out

by dust and grit from

the concrete buildings destroyed

by air strikes

little kids are crying

out for their

mothers, uncles, fathers

food, water

now AI called

Habsora which means "gospel" which means "good
    news"

is being used to progress from 50

    targets

a year to 100 a day

and expands the precision

to the exact # of

people in a room the science of

genocide is so

successful that no one

knows where safety is but pilots

know

exactly where you are

the four premature babies are

decomposing in hospital

the small coffins

are the heaviest

INSPECTION

for Doug Ballard

Today on my inspection tour
around Delano I stopped by Al's
Old & New Book Store which I
haven't I'm ashamed to say been
in since they moved from their old
location a few doors down. The
building used to be a Safeway
Grocery store a while back. The
current owner purchased the store
from a high school classmate of
mine, Andy Woodward's mom. Both
are gone now but it was a great
experience and I will be back
soon. On a positive note I did
purchase a book about Delano by
another classmate from West
High 1966. Pat O'Connor. I posted
a picture of it also.

Dawn and the

cloud-curdled sea
waving to us
with a mystifying
message more ancient
than the angular stone
bracing the world for
the cry of survivors
breaking the waves
only to be dragged
back by the coastal islands
reaching out in their feral way
for the wild, sleep-deprived
devil, that man
spitting out lie after lie.

THE BOOK

She placed her hand
on the hand
on the cover
of the book. It was
a perfect fit. The gift
meant as a treasure
was cherished. Another
perfect fit. But the birds
and Kunitz have
died. She did not
but only disappeared
as one child
from another, exhausted,
from trying so hard.

The anticipation

the night before

                    forecast of first snow

of winter

                    I remember as a kid

I now feel

                    as an old poet

in my cellular structure

                    something to look

forward to
as a replacement

                    for the dungeon

of late fall

PART III

"Tho' my errors nd wrecks lie around me."

-Ezra Pound, *New Cantos*

I am from a small town
in the middle of the U.S. I was bored
so, I went to a large city
on the west coast. Then I worked
in cafés washing dishes
and scrubbing floors. I was seen
by a man who smiled kindly.
We talked and he promised me
a better life. It was a lie.
I believe now most men
lie to me. I tried to
escape many times. I was
used and brutalized in so many
ways. I am ashamed. Do you know
the feeling of shame? Of being naked
in front of several men
until one, or more than one, wants you
for an hour, a day, a week?
But I am not there now
except in my nightmares which are
constant, sometimes during the
day. Now I am a man,
fourteen years old, two since
being taken. A woman
found me as I was scrambling
through a trash bin behind a

grocery store. With one can
of tomato soup, which I kept,
she took me to a safe place.
I cried for days on the floor
of that place, with a pillow
to hold. In time, I could sit on a chair.
In time I had the heart tattoo, my brand,
removed from my gleaming white ass.

MOTHERS

-Gaza, 2023

Will their wellness?
Settle their memories?
The cost might
not be proportional
as you remember
the pain of finding
a familiar looking
hand in the grey
dust covering your
head, and so far,
your whole life.
You pick up the hand,
put it in the
embroidered cloth
bag you and your
neighbors carry
for such things now.
It's the same beautiful
bag your mother
used for oranges, lettuce,
and strawberries
on market day
near Al Shifa. Now
it's still for your family –
arms hands legs (your
3-month-old sister) feet
and hope, in your

ten-year-old way,
that the mothers
will claim their wellness,
recall the magic memories.
Meanwhile, you stumble over
sharp and crumbling blocks
of concrete and shout
the name of your Baba.

HARD BOUND BOOK

The older I get
the more I want
to buy hard bound
books, hold them as
a guard against sequential
loneliness.
And the older I get
the more expensive
those books become,
but the solid sanctity
of the hard gem
with words is more than
worth it. I turn each page,
with the touch of first love.
I caress the print on the warm
paper, skimming the flesh
of the loved. The clerk
looks at me suspiciously,
as if some perversion
is taking place. I lay
the book on the counter
to assure him that this
is a legitimate and legal
encounter. He takes my money
but the book is no longer
on the counter. No one
took it to place it in a bag,
no one is near me. The book

is gone like a child from my life,
taken to a dark island
off the coast of Maine with no phone,
no way to communicate with my son
or daughter. I looked away for
only an instant, some distraction
in the midst of the shelves.
But that's all it takes.

"BARBIE" AND PRIJEDOR*

Before I saw the film,
a friend told me
they thought
it was all about
sex, a 2 hour +
porno flick.

       No dietary concerns
       2nd floor is fine
       No disability issues

He said, "Barbie's blouse
was usually unbuttoned
just enough," aroused. "Damn!"

       He will check with his wife
       Over 2 billion in global sales
       Like "Cats" it was just in front of the world
       Like Prijedor it was too late discovered

Another friend, years earlier, laid out all his daughter's old
Barbie collection, all naked, to see how they had changed
over the years, as a curious joke

he laid them out on his long oak kitchen table
side by side each one stared off in the distance
away from us – thinking of only a week before
of school of family of marriage of children

this is ethnic cleansing

*Prijedor, a town in northwestern Bosnia and Herzegovina, was the site of
one of the earliest attempts, in 1992, by Serb military and political forces
to set up detention camps for non-Serbs. The several camps became notorious
for the brutal acts of torture, rape, and murders during the early years of the
tragic and genocidal war initiated by the Serbs to "ethnically cleanse" Bosnia
and Herzegovina and establish a Serb-only entity.

SHORT HISTORY OF WAR

Say they use white
phosphorus, does that
make a difference?

Before dawn the sky
has fallen into a
dead sleep. The buildings

gone from solid stone
to rocks to gravel
and without water

there is no coffee. Soon
we'll drink the sea
and join the disappeared.

ice cube

i place one
ice cube in the dirt
at the base
of my orchids

the purple ones
in full regalia
the opposite
of stone

but why would you
care – your orchid
is nothing but
a couple of sticks

stuck in the pot
waving at the flies
come around for
this reason

THE EDGE

We take our grandson
        to the edge of this country
he is a year old
        and stumbles through the chill water
of the Atlantic for the first
        time in his evolving life
he is tired, hungry so the experience
        is not as thrilling as for us –
that happens often with our expectations
        for others – so much anticipation
we will have to salvage
        and disappointment we will transform
into indoor fun, tiny chunks of cheese,
        small spoonsful of banana, blockading the stairway
survival of small green plants
        wherever we live, with whomever
it is always life on the edge
        and today there are warnings of rip tides
you know those advisories in your life
        as personal and chaotically arranged
or miscalculated as if you multiplied instead
        of divided – our grandson's eyes
are serious, questioning this whole adventure
        as we stay away from the dangers
of the water not wanting to fall off or be swept out
        we hold onto each other led by the child
tired and hungry in his wise age or natural needs

for survival translated from the savage
we edge away from the dangers of the salt and sea
move inward to the questions of each
estuarial day.

HOUSE OF SAND

Your tribal
colleagues
confuse life
as is
with life
as it is.
That could
be lethal
for such
a house.
When the owner,
past living,
seizes ambition
and, on the
other hand,
at the climax
chokes on the
surrounding pattern
of dunes, from which
the kingdom
is made, there will be a coup.
Like your colleagues
you will wonder about
marriage and fidelity,
motives and mantras
when the owner
shows up – out of nowhere –
and erases his house

in fear that you might
blossom so beautifully
from the sand that fragrance
breathing like Paris perfume
into your lungs forever.

"WHAT'S THE HURRY ON YOU?"

This is a quote translated
from the Irish. Roughly
it means: "The hug is free but
anything else will cost you."
Not really. I made that up
but the title is real. And
a powerful reading of
our persistent drama,
the rhetoric of our staged life.

What's the hurry on you?
It's the opposite of dysania,
a state of finding it
difficult to leave bed
in the morning. There is
our unneeded rush to get
across town, across the room,
feel the quick skin but only
the quick, any more will cost you.

We always need one more word.
What's the hurry "on."? What is
sitting on your heart? Are these
the gentle words or the rocks
of Aran? Now we are on the
islands with eight foot tall
rock stalls to protect the cattle
from weeks of storms.
What's the hurry on now?

20 CELEBRITIES WHO MARRIED
UGLY SPOUSES

Today Flotilla III left various
European ports all destined
For the harbor in Gaza. Their goal
Is to break the illegal blockade
Keeping three million human beings
Incarcerated in the world's largest
Outdoor prison. About half
Of those prisoners are children.

Celebrities float into and out of our
Lives daily. Some of us regard them
As a touchstone or a port, a refuge for
Our own thoughtless and violent predatory
Living. Twenty is a nice round number like:
The victim had 20 rounds fired into her.

PUTTING DOWN

How she withstood
His care, aware
Or not. It will
Always be a question
For me. It always
Will seem more like
Treatment than care.
Or mistreatment.
Maybe a love song
Gone terribly wrong.

WRITING ABOUT OUR
SCANDALOUS SECRETS

Because at our age,
seventy or older,
we begin farting,
unconsciously,
not on purpose.

It's a biological
fact. You can
look it up. It's a signal,
a small noise
from mother's nature
to let the rest of you know
we are still around.

SCHERZO

You can laugh if you
wish but this is no
joke. It's a musical
term for something
partially funny or
light spirited. As
things turned out, you
heard exquisite dentelated
lace chords gazing out
from the string section
at the end of a cultural
institution withered into
complete token stiff black
and as charred as the regime
town mentioned in "Schindler's List"
as Budysin. Soon you also hear
your own scherzo coming from the
tiger cages where you have stood for hours.
The tour director never mentioned this.

IS THERE LIFE BEYOND
THE LIFE BEYOND?

I'm not Buddhist but the title
Of this poem finds me posing
As a monk, orange robe, usually
Quite silent except when chanting
Or when I am hungry. And I have
Noticed the summer is dark because
We keep the blinds and curtains closed
Especially on the south side of the
Temple. The great war has changed so much
When considering making a life or love beyond.
We have only to look around. We will walk
Carefully from here on, through a flowered
Forest, overwhelmed with invasive species.

ADIAN IN ISTANBUL

July 27, 2022

endowed with wonder
it's so rare
or maybe the eyes
bold and black

to watch ahead
night or day
pulling in the world
black and bold

WHELMED

You reach a certain age
and nearly every conversation
is seen as flirtatious.

It's exhausting watching
your step and each sentence
to the waitress or waiter.

I'm told it's all in the pronouns
people use to identify. My face
reveals the confusion so my

daughter advises me just to
write more, every day. Stay
indoors with my wife, away from crowds.

"the weather report of
cooler promises"

---- overheard somewhere, 2022

you say your yellow heart will give you trouble
some of my best friends tell me
these are the greatest of times, we are free
to dig the ditches, drain the swamps, build the walls
and our dream homes for others to buy
we are all odd

in our own spectacular, low brow,
manipulative or generous ways

we are so evocative of the well-
known life
the erotic similarity equivalent to common sense
without the common and you still say your yellow
heart will give you

trouble
erotic (again) and as deadly as Srebrenica, silver city, in
the country
without articles, with the produce market in the empty
town square, and the one Muslim family that returned,
the coffee shop
we have a coffee but the four of us are all nervous, the
rifles, do you hate me?
do you believe in weather reports or predictions? are
your promises warm or

cool? you like the ugly and
expensive
religious status with the facial features promised

but instead comes just as a full blank stare,
your assaulted ten-year-old life is a

                           mimed

wordplay
and we are all surrounded by the crimes themselves

AMBER ALERT

The missing has an alert
that is broadcast across
the country. My cellphone
vibrates like all the others
in this café. Do we know
the person? Did they not show
up for work or school? Is there
a description of the sedan,
old model, rust along the
passenger side? Then the alert
appears on the monitor at
the south end of the counter
as several of us have stopped
drinking our coffee. A blurred
photo of somebody, victim (?),
perpetrator (?) On my end of
the counter, fresh coffee is
being poured by the waitress --
pouring perfectly while watching
the monitor that seems a mile
away. The look on her face
is not neutral, by miles. She has a hand
in this pot. I figure she'll
ditch this job in an hour
and meet her daughter and boyfriend
north of Salt Lake. Then, in spite
of the alert, that ancient rusting sedan

will try to cross from Montana into
Canada, like Chief Joseph. He came
so close but could fight no more
forever. We do that to people. Force them
to try an escape only to catch up just short,
their arm in the air, indigenous, and frozen.

THE SEARCH

How old is your hand?
Or your blue eyes?
Has your left leg
been growing older over
the years more than your right?
For answers to these
questions, first wash
the blood and urine
from your shirt
and rethink the naked body
floating across the
sky. It's a kind of
liberation, a crossing
of the Arizona desert,
the Drina River,
the southside street,
finding the empty
water bottles and the
deteriorating clothes you
recognize from the village goodbye.
So, none of this helps with the
answers? Then, I am not your woman.

PHANTOM

And I approached the pond.
I heard some strange sounds
like harsh voices on a
dark Halloween night. I walked closer
toward the pond, stepping into the mud
showing tracks of deer, racoons,
and sketchy birds coming for water. Then
I saw the shadows of two snakes
each struggling to swallow the same
bullfrog. Fang to fang, one limp
frog leg dangling down, each predator
twisting and flipping in the fire of my
flashlight. Which one needed the food
more than the other? This was no time
for declaring victory, for calling the kids at home
to tell them dinner was on the way. Each snake
was still using all possible energy
to get the other to release
but neither one gave way,
they slapped through the mud
toward the water. This was their
vocation, the god's baptism – to be so
vigilant and quiet, each day, without
formal training, to fight, to swallow
even as they edged into the water,
another dark world, end of evening,
end of the opera.

the cure

yes ((even the least
of these can stand
alone
            above the tower of Krakow
the lonely one
will break your
                    heart
but then you are
                    welcome
to cradle the beautiful
windows
            of any cathedral you can find
            in this city

there will be   of course
consequences for your example

                        to others
there is one dignified
choice
the sweet opposite of
                        (liberated love)
the poison that heals

STARRY NIGHT

So, to let you know
The sky here is full
Of ash because of the
Constant shelling and fires.

My patient's lungs are
Suffering the shadow
Syndrome causing breathing
Difficulty and tumors.

Everyone with any strength
Writes their memoir with
Longings for the salt air
From any sea to wash

Over them, or to die.
Seagulls, conjured by the
Imaginations of the sick,
Snag the splintered

Bones of the washed up,
The done for, making another
Meal. Here the sky is very full,
Wanted you to get the news.

O TASTE AND SMELL

It is the hell of waiting on Thanksgiving Day.

For a nuclear "accident" in Ukraine at Zaporizhzhia.

Ironic how we pray for peace and say you are in our
   thoughts.

The taste of the meal is a reminder of childhood but
   not of what could be.

At our table the ages ranged from eighty-one to three
   months.

At the end, we thank each other, say goodbye, at least
   we are too warm.

MODERN WARFARE

Your floor is made of
dust and a final coating
of my breath. Outside
the wind is fifty mph
from the north. The skin
of the house is curling
up and is ripped from the
bones as if to magnify
the torture. From the drone
you see your target, but it
looks more like a wedding.
Your two failed, thru the crosshairs,
so, why not this one.

ANAPHORA #1

Text primary care to sustain life beyond the wall.

Text primary care to reach el otro lado.

Text primary care to seize, to seize the courage to
cross another mind field.

Text primary care in case you have something
important to say.

Text primary care and preach the revolution from
motherhood.

Text primary care to observe the primary, secondary,
and tertiary graves of the masses whose
clothes you finally recognize. They are number
3432 in the loose-leaf binder near Tuzla.

Text primary care when you are done, done with it all.

BOSNA 3

This winter
there are changes in life
along the rocks
of the Neretva, beneath
the stecci, the blue
water. You make
coffee, the pastime,
as we sit close
to each other
and you lean against
my shoulder as I fall
into convalescence,
and shake off the snow
from Stolac accumulating
around my neck
and throat. There is nothing
further to decide so
we must call this part:
the beginning.

Michael Poage has been writing since 1967 and this book is his eighteenth collection of poems. He has lived and/or worked in Latvia, Mexico, Gaza, Bosnia & Herzegovina, as well as the U.S. He has worked as a grocery clerk, manual laborer, teaching in a two-room school in Montana, operated a sheep ranch in western Montana, and has taught English language usage and English Literature to international students virtually in Thailand and in-person in Bosnia and at Wichita State University, Wichita, Kansas. He served as the Poet- in-Residence at Dzemal Bijedic University (2017-18). He lives with his wife, Dr. Gretchen Eick, writer, teacher, activist, in Wichita, Kansas.

This project was made possible, in part, by generous support from the Osage Arts Community.

Osage Arts Community provides temporary time, space and support for the creation of new artistic works in a retreat format, serving creative people of all kinds — visual artists, composers, poets, fiction and nonfiction writers. Located on a 152-acre farm in an isolated rural mountainside setting in Central Missouri and bordered by ¾ of a mile of the Gasconade River, OAC provides residencies to those working alone, as well as welcoming collaborative teams, offering living space and workspace in a country environment to emerging and mid-career artists. For more information, visit us at www.osageac.org

Osage Arts Community